ENDANGERED!

TIGERS

Marc Tyler Nobleman

Marshall Cavendish
Benchmark
New York

Marshall Cavendish Benchmark
99 White Plains Road
Tarrytown, New York 10591
www.marshallcavendish.us

Editor: Karen Ang
Publisher: Michelle Bisson
Art Director: Anahid Hamparian
Series Designer: Elynn Cohen
Cover Design by Kay Petronio

Library of Congress Cataloging-in-Publication Data
Nobleman, Marc Tyler.
Tigers / Marc Tyler Nobleman.
p. cm. — (Endangered!)
Summary: "Describes the characteristics, behavior, and plight of
endangered tiger species, and what people can do to help"—Provided by publisher.
Includes bibliographical references and index.
ISBN 978-0-7614-2986-9
1. Tigers—Juvenile literature. 2. Endangered species—Juvenile literature.
I. Title. II. Series.
QL737.C23N63 2009
599.756—dc22
2008017553
Front cover: A Bengal tiger
Back cover: A white Bengal tiger (top)
A Siberian tiger cub (bottom)

Photo research by Pamela Mitsakos
Front cover: Tiago Jorge da Silva Estima / Shutterstock

The photographs in this book are used by permission and through the courtesy of:
Shutterstock: R. Gino Santa Maria, back cover (top); David Crippen Photography, back cover (bottom);
Chad Littlejohn, 6; Stephen Meese, 7; iconex, 15; Tatiana Popova, 23; Andrey Ushakov, 29 (right); Snowleopard1,
44. Alamy: Peter Steiner, 1; Peter Oxford, 12, 39; Terry Whitaker, 13; Sharad Bhandhari, 18; David Hosking, 19;
India Images, 20; D. Fernandez & M. Peck, 22; Tom Brakefield, 24; Stuart Greenhalgh, 26; Heather Angel, 27;
Peter Nicholson, 30; Michael Weber, 34. Corbis: Frans Lanting, 4; Tom Brakefield, 9. © Fine Art Photographic
Library, 10; © Hulton-Deutsch Collection, 36; © R.P.G./Yevgeny Kondakov, 37. Minden: Francois Savigny, 16; ZSSD,
32. AP Images: Peng Zhangqing, 29 (left); Richard Vogel, 40; Chris Fontaine, 41; Sherwin Crasto, 43.

Printed in China
1 2 3 4 5 6

Contents

1

The Hunters Become the Hunted

A large boar walks through an Asian forest. Suddenly, it senses that it is not alone. At first, it does not see or hear anything unusual, but a moment later, a beautiful and powerful animal creeps out of the leafy shadows. The panicked boar takes barely a few steps before the big cat pounces. Just as the tiger reaches for the boar, the sound of a gunshot shatters the air. The boar is spared—but the

An adult tiger prepares to take down its prey. Humans and their weapons are the only things that can stop this master predator.

No two sets of tiger stripes are alike. In fact, the stripes on either side of a tiger's body are different from each other.

tiger is not. As the boar runs back into the safety of the forest, the tiger lies on the ground dying. Once a master **predator**, the big cat is now the victim of a more dangerous hunter—a human **poacher**.

As the largest living members of the cat family, tigers have no natural predators, except for humans. Both accidentally and on pupose, human beings have killed a huge number of tigers in a short amount of time. People did this for profit, for land, for sport, or for protection. An estimated 100,000 tigers roamed through Asia in the 1800s and 1900s. By 2005, however, only 5,000 to 7,000 tigers exist in the wild. Kept in zoos, circuses, and by private owners, it is now likely that there are more tigers living in **captivity** than in the wild.

Wild tigers make their homes in parts of India, China, Russia, Indonesia, Malaysia, Nepal, Bangladesh, Myanmar, Bhutan, Thailand, Laos, Vietnam, Cambodia, and North

During the twentieth century, the worldwide population of wild tigers decreased by about 95 percent. Without conservation efforts to protect them, wild tigers may soon become extinct.

Korea. Within those countries, tigers inhabit a broad range of environments. This includes wet forests, such as the tropical rainforests of the Indonesian island of Sumatra, and dry forests, like the thorn forests of north-western India. Wild tigers also prowl through the tall grass at the base of the Himalayas, which are the large mountains along the India-Tibet border. Some tigers venture high up into the mountains as well. People have spotted tiger tracks in the snow at elevations of 9,840 feet (3,000 meters).

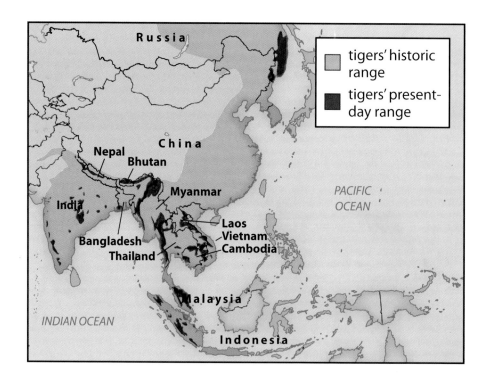

Some tigers are used to the cold and snowy climates in the north.

The land through which they roam now may seem like a very large territory, but it represents only 7 percent of the former range of tigers. At one time, tigers also lived in many other Asian nations including Pakistan and Singapore, but now they are considered **extinct** in those regions. Tigers are scattered throughout the continent in groups that are shrinking every year.

2

Humans versus Tigers

A natural tiger habitat must have three main features: a steady water supply, a large population of large prey (such as deer and boar), and a lot of forest **vegetation** or tall grass so that it can hunt that prey successfully. Without these things, tiger populations either die out or move to other areas, often entering human developments.

This painting shows a traditional tiger hunt in India. For hundreds of years, tigers were hunted for sport.

CROSSING PATHS

Tigers need a hunting territory of 8 square miles to 60 square miles (21 square kilometers to 155 square kilometers). However, if prey is hard to find, they may hunt across an area that is nearly 200 square miles (518 square km). Unfortunately, tiger habitats overlap an area where human populations are increasing quickly. People who live in tiger habitats are constantly expanding their settlements, which cuts into tiger territory. Forests in Asia are being cut down at an alarming rate to make way for more villages and roads. This squeezes animals—including tigers—into smaller

This tiger is traveling along a road often used by local villagers. As wild tiger habitats continue to disappear, the chance that humans and tigers will cross paths increases.

and smaller areas. This also leads to confrontations between man and beast.

Tigers generally avoid human contact. Some people who live in tiger habitats say that they have never seen a live tiger or heard one roar. Even some scientists who study tigers in the wild rarely—if ever—spot one.

Though tigers do kill people at times, scientists believe that only a small percentage of tigers are man-eaters. The more contact a tiger has with humans, the bolder it could become. Sometimes tigers attack people in retaliation. If a tiger feels threatened it will most likely fight back. Like other females in the animal kingdom, tigresses (female tigers) will defend their **cubs**. When adult

Tiger attacks on humans usually occur when the tiger feels threatened. A tigress may attack to protect her cubs.

tigers attack humans, their cubs may copy that behavior.

At other times, tigers attack out of desperation. When their natural prey is in short supply due to bad weather, human hunting, or **deforestation**, tigers may go after people. If a tiger grabs a domesticated animal such as a goat, sheep, cow, or dog and a human tries to scare it off, the tiger may lash out. Tigers that are sick, injured, or old are also more likely to attack humans. In those conditions, tigers may not be fast enough to capture their regular prey. Humans, however, are slower than a tiger's regular prey, and certainly slower than a tiger. A tiger can run 35 miles per hour (56 km per hour), while an average human's top speed is less than 20 miles per hour (32 km per hour).

MISCONCEPTIONS

Part of the problem tigers face are misconceptions—or misunderstanding—by humans. Some people do not realize that humans are partly to blame for many tiger attacks. Instead they see tigers as either **pests** or bloodthirsty

Tigers can damage or lose teeth due to age, accidents, or fights with other animals. A tiger with broken or missing teeth has a harder time catching and holding its usual prey and may turn to attacking humans.

animals that should be killed before they can harm any people. Because tigers tend to have this ferocious reputation, people often feel they can shoot a tiger on sight even if it is not behaving aggressively. Many people do this even though it is against the law.

Tigers survived for tens of thousands of years without human intervention, or interference, but they were nearly wiped out in the past one hundred years because of it. To save tigers, people must actually save more than tigers. They must save tiger prey and tiger habitats, too.

3

The Life of
a Tiger

Tigers are the largest members of the family of big cats that includes lions and leopards. Adult male tigers can weigh more than 600 pounds (272 kilograms), though they typically weigh between 350 pounds (160 kg) to 500 pounds (230 kg). On average, they are 8 feet (2.4 meters) to 10 feet (3 m) long and are 3 feet (.9 m) high at the shoulder. Males are generally larger than females.

Tigers will scratch and rub up against trees to mark their territory.

HUNTING FOR FOOD

Tigers are also the biggest meat-eating land mammals. Nearly any animal in a tiger habitat can be prey for the big cats. Tigers have been known to take down animals as large as elephants and snatch up critters as small as mice. A tiger's diet depends on its environment, but it can include wild boar, wild ox, deer, monkeys, birds, and fish. Some tigers have even eaten other tigers.

Even though they are very big, tigers are quiet enough and fast enough to sneak up on their prey.

A tiger's stripes help it hide in tall grasses.

Rather than rely on running to capture prey, a tiger uses **stealth**. As it quietly follows an animal through the brush, tall grasses, or other plant life, the tiger's stripes **camouflage** it. You might think that orange and black stripes would only make a tiger stand out against green grass and leaves. However, the stripes actually break up the outline of the tiger's body as it creeps through the grass. This way the tiger can blend in.

When it is close enough to catch an animal, the tiger leaps with its long, powerful hind legs. Tigers prefer to attack from behind since it is more of a surprise. Despite their large size and their powerful bodies, tigers do not catch every animal they pursue. A tiger may make between ten and twenty attempts on different animals before succeeding. Once the prey is dead, a tiger often drags the **carcass** into the brush so other animals will not try to take it or eat from it.

Tigers prefer larger prey because it provides food for a longer period of time. This means that they will not have

Tigers can climb up trees to eat or hide their prey or to rest on very large branches. When resting on a large branch, a tiger can easily jump down upon unsuspecting prey.

to use up a lot of energy to hunt again right away. A tiger may make a kill only once or twice a week. It will return to feed on the leftovers of one kill for as many days as the meat lasts. A tiger may eat up to 80 pounds (36 kg) of meat at once!

THE LIFE CYCLE

Some tigers are nocturnal, which means they are most active at night. This is because they live in climates in which it can get too hot to move around a lot during the day. A tiger's night vision is six times as powerful as a human's.

Though tigers are usually solitary creatures that live by themselves, they do socialize at times. Scientists have observed more than one tiger hunting together, often a mother and her cubs. On occasion, more than one tiger will share meat from a kill, though usually only one eats at a time. Naturally, adult tigers also live together for a short while in order to have babies.

After a pregnancy that lasts about three and a half months, a female tiger gives birth to two to three cubs. Each small cub weighs about 3 pounds (1.3 kg). Until they are around two years old, the cubs will stay with their mother. She teaches them survival skills like hunting.

When they are ready, the tigers go off on their own. With luck, they will grow into large adults that breed more tiger cubs. In the wild, a tiger's lifespan can be ten to fifteen years. However, with poaching, habitat destruction, and limited prey, few wild tigers ever live that long.

Besides learning survival skills from their mothers, tiger cubs also learn from each other. Play fighting teaches them how to defend their territory or food.

PET TIGERS

An estimated 6,000 to 7,000 tigers are kept as pets by private individuals who are not associated with zoos, wildlife parks or **preserves**, or other **conservation** efforts. While this may seem to save these tigers from the hardships that their relatives in the wild may face, in most cases, pet tigers suffer more. Besides the fact that it is dangerous for the humans, pet tigers usually do not receive the care that they deserve. Often, the pet tigers are not given enough room to roam. Pet tigers that are rescued from these homes are often underfed, unhealthy, and do not know how to interact with humans and other tigers.

Most tigers that are kept as pets are stuck in small cages that do not give them room to hunt and run around.

4

Tigers of Many Stripes

From biggest to smallest, the six known surviving tiger subspecies—or types within a species—are the Amur (or Siberian), Bengal, Indochinese, South China, Sumatran, and Malayan. Though their size and locations vary, they are not extremely different from one another. All tigers are considered endangered species because their wild populations are close to disappearing.

An Indochinese tiger attempts to cross a stream. Tigers will often swim across short distances.

Like all tigers, Siberian, or Amur, tigers have large paws with very sharp claws. A tiger uses its paws to take down prey and to interact with other tigers.

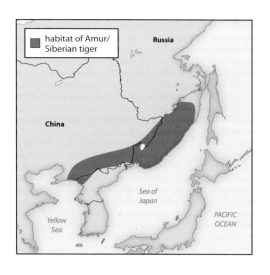

habitat of Amur/
Siberian tiger

Russia

China

Sea of
Japan

Yellow
Sea

PACIFIC
OCEAN

THE AMUR OR SIBERIAN TIGER

The Amur tiger is the largest of the tigers. A full grown male may be 13 feet (4 m) long and weigh more than 600 pounds (272 kg). Though they are orange and black like most tigers, Amur tigers are the palest of the tigers.

Most wild Amur tigers live in eastern parts of Russia. A few live in northeastern China. Cool forests are the main habitat for these types of tigers, but they can also withstand the cold and snow that hits these regions every year.

Scientists estimate that in the 1940s there were only around 40 Amur tigers left in the wild. This was due to loss of habitat and over-hunting. Conservation efforts have helped to increase the Amur tiger populations, and today there are around 400 in the wild.

THE BENGAL TIGER

Sometimes called the Indian tiger, an adult Bengal tiger can grow to be about 9 feet (2.7 m) long and weigh around 550 pounds (250 kg). They live in wet and dry forests in India, Nepal, Bhutan, Myanmar, and Bangladesh. Approximately 3,000 to 4,500 Bengal tigers remain in the wild today. Bengal tigers make up nearly two-thirds of the existing wild tiger population.

Most Bengal tigers live in forests, but some can be found in coastal areas.

Though their numbers are larger than some other tiger populations, Bengal tigers are still in danger. Poaching, habitat destruction, and competing with humans for prey have reduced

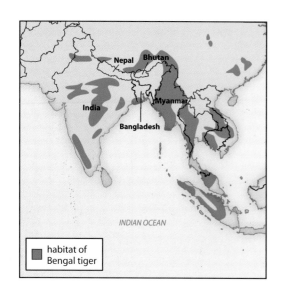

habitat of
Bengal tiger

the tigers' numbers. However, conservation efforts in India and Nepal are helping to preserve Bengal tiger populations.

THE INDOCHINESE TIGER

Most wild Indochinese tigers live in Thailand, but there are also populations in Myanmar, Cambodia, Laos, Vietnam, and southern China. Adult males can grow to be about 8 feet (2.4 m) long and around 350 pounds (158.7 kg) in weight. Unfortunately, scientists do not

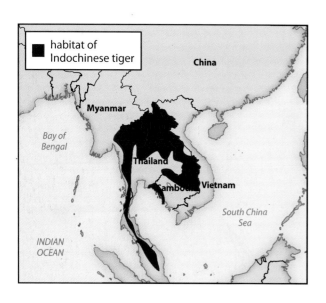

habitat of
Indochinese tiger

have a lot of information about these tigers. One reason is because the wild tigers live in areas that are hard to reach and observe. Today, scientists estimate that there are only about 1,220 to 1,785 Indochinese tigers remaining in the wild.

THE SOUTH CHINA TIGER

Despite its name, the South China tiger was found in central and eastern China. While some believe that fewer than thirty South China tigers exist in the wild, Chinese officials have not seen one for more than twenty years. So it is possible that this tiger is already extinct.

This photograph of a wild South China tiger was taken in the late 1970s. Since then, none of these tigers have been spotted in their natural habitats.

WHITE TIGERS

White tigers are rare in the wild. The last time one was reported in the wild was 1951. All known white tigers are Bengal or part Bengal. White tigers have blue eyes, instead of the yellow that other tigers have. White tigers are not purely white—they usually have brown stripes.

THE SUMATRAN TIGER

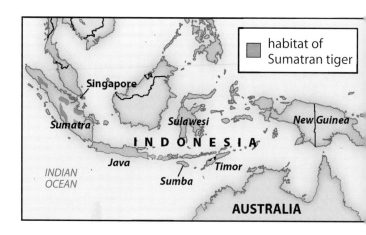

The Sumatran tiger is the smallest and darkest of the tigers. These tigers used to live on different islands in Indonesia. Unfortunately, today the only wild Sumatran tigers live on Sumatra, which is an island of Indonesia. Scientists estimate that there are fewer than 400 Sumatran tigers left in the wild.

The Sumatran tiger has a ruff, or gathering of fur, around its neck. Adults can be around 7 feet (2.1 m) long and weigh around 165 pounds (74.8 kg) and 300 pounds (136 kg).

The fur in a Sumatran tiger's ruff is long and mostly white.

THE MALAYAN TIGER

The Malayan tiger was classified as an Indochinese tiger until 2004, when scientists discovered differences between the tigers' genes (the parts of cells that determine characteristics).

The Malayan tiger's body is similar to the Indochinese tiger's, and it is the approximate size of the Sumatran tiger. The Malayan tiger lives in the southern part of the Malay Peninsula, which includes Thailand. At least 500 tigers remain in the wild today.

A young Malayan tiger hides in a tropical forest in Thailand.

EXTINCT TIGERS

The three subspecies of tigers that became extinct in the twentieth century were the Bali, Caspian, and Javan tigers. The Bali was native to the Indonesian island it was named after. The Javan also lived exclusively on an

Indonesian island, Java. The Caspian was found in countries including Afghanistan, Iran, Turkey, and Russia.

Scientists cannot say for sure exactly when these tigers became extinct. However, in 1937, a tiger that was believed to be the last Bali was killed. The last Caspian tiger was seen in the wild in 1972. By the 1980s, the Javan tiger was gone, too. Over the years, people have reported seeing some of these species, but they are most likely mistaken. In some cases, the habitats where these tigers lived have too much human development and would no longer be able to support the tigers.

TOO LITTLE TOO LATE

In the past, people made few organized efforts to save the now-extinct tigers. This is especially true of the Bali tiger, which was the first of the three now-extinct tigers to die out. Local governments were unwilling to stop human developments in the tiger habitats. Additionally, laws did not protect the tigers from being poached. In the 1940s, land was set aside for the Javan tiger, but the land area was too small and set up too late to succeed.

5

Saving the Tigers

Tigers are a sign of a healthy habitat. A tiger's presence shows that the habitat has enough food and water to nourish such a large animal. Without tigers, that environment would undergo a change. For example, the populations of its prey—such as deer, antelope, wild boar—could grow out of control. When tigers disappear from their natural habitats, the habitat suffers as the balance of nature is disrupted.

A young cub plays with its mother's tail. Many people hope that conservation efforts will help this wild tiger live a long and healthy life in its natural habitat.

THE HUMAN PROBLEM

In every major way, humans were—and continue to be— the reason why tigers are endangered. Some experts trace the beginning of the tigers' decline to the nine- teenth century, when India was under British control. Men commonly hunted tigers as a test of bravery. It was a fashionable sport and the trophy was the head or skin of

Tiger hunters did not care about how many tigers they killed or what would happen to the tigers in the future.

one of the world's largest and fiercest beasts. At the time, very few people paid attention to how this over-hunting would affect the tigers' future survival.

Poaching, or illegal hunting, continues to be a serious problem. Even though tiger hunting is now illegal worldwide, and even though the Convention for International Trade on Endangered Species (CITES) has banned the sale of any tiger products, the countries that pass these laws do not always enforce them. Sometimes this is because the wildlife departments do not have the staff or

These Russian officers display the tiger skins they took from poachers who illegally hunted Siberian tigers.

the budget to enforce the laws. Also, sometimes the laws do not apply to tigers found outside of protected areas like reserves or national parks.

In 1973, India started a conversation program called Project Tiger. This program created reserves around the country and led to an increase in the tiger population. However, just before the program was launched, people scrambled to kill tigers before the animals went under protection, further reducing the tiger populations.

Tiger Parts

People still kill tigers for sport, as well as for other reasons. Poachers sell tiger body parts for use in traditional Asian medicine. According to some beliefs, nearly every part of a tiger can help cure some kind of illness—from toothaches to pimples to serious diseases like malaria. For example, tiger tails are used to treat skin diseases. Tiger bones are in high demand. The bones are crushed to a powder and added to mixtures that supposedly have great healing qualities.

While this traditional medicine is effective for some people, scientific studies have not shown that tiger parts have real health benefits. Tiger conservationists want to be as respectful as possible of traditional beliefs, but not at the expense of the tigers' lives. They suggest natural alternatives to tiger parts, often involving herbs.

Tigers are also killed to be used as decoration. Certain cultures wear tiger skins in ceremonies, while others use them in their homes as rugs or wall hangings. Because worldwide demand for tiger skins is often high, poachers can gain a lot for them. One dead tiger can earn a hunter around $15,000.

Tiger paws and bones can be found in many marketplaces throughout Asia.

Habitat Destruction

Forests around the world are constantly cut down to provide wood products such as building materials and paper. When humans clear Asian forests, tigers have less room to roam and fewer areas in which to hunt. Deforestation also drives off tiger prey, leaving the tigers with nothing to

Deforestation—and the roads used to take the wood away— destroys wild tigers' natural habitat.

eat. Tigers cannot always easily relocate to where prey is more abundant because the tigers would have to cross human populations to get there.

Loss of habitat also affects how healthy future tiger generations will be. There are fewer wild tigers and they are forced to live in limited areas that are far away from other wild tiger populations. As a result, tigers end up breeding within the same small group again and again. This weakens the gene pool, which means that the cubs born from these breedings are not as strong or healthy as their parents and grandparents. Conservationists are trying to establish corridors between these "pockets" of tiger populations. These corridors would allow tigers to travel safely from one suitable habitat to another. There they can breed and interact with a wider selection of tigers.

CONSERVATION EFFORTS

Zoos are a valuable force in tiger conservation for many reasons. Besides providing tigers with safe living areas with adequate food and water, zoos also enable tigers to breed properly. Tigers kept in zoos—whether or not they

Two scientists set up cameras in a forest in Thailand. The camera can be used to catch poachers or to monitor wild tiger activity. This information can help conservation efforts to protect the tigers.

breed—are watched closely and are provided with good healthcare, medication, and surgeries when needed. Zoos also teach large numbers of people about the problems tigers face and what can be done to help them. Many wildlife parks and zoos take a portion of the money earned from admissions and souvenirs and give it to programs that protect wild tigers.

Many conservation programs involve tracking wild tigers. Scientists sometimes use radio collars to keep track of wild tigers. These devices send signals so the scientists can follow tiger movement. Learning more about tiger habits will help scientists figure out ways to protect the tigers.

Preserving tiger habitats is key to the tigers' survival. Many Asian nations have set aside land specifically for tigers. On this land, tigers cannot be hunted or harmed. Scientists are also using satellite technology to map areas that could be good habitats for tigers in the future. At times, entire human villages have been moved away from protected tiger habitats in order to reduce tiger-human problems.

THE OTHER SIDE

While nearly everyone agrees that it is important to protect wildlife, sometimes people feel
they have no choice but to do things that hurt
the tigers. For example, many people who live
near tigers are poor and rely on their natural
surroundings to make a living. They need to
cut down forests to grow crops or sell the
wood. Tigers that kill farmers' livestock are
seen as pests. So when tigers compete with
their way of life, many people have little choice
but to kill the big cats in order to survive.

*An Indian woman scoops up
water from her village's nearly
empty well. Her village is right
next to a tiger preserve that
the villagers are not allowed
to enter. Unfortunately, the
closest stream—which they
need for drinking water—is
located in the preserve.*

Programs created to help tigers are expen-
sive to run. Some countries do not want to
take part in these programs because no one
profits from them—except for tigers. Additionally, saving tigers
means limiting human developments. To many, this is bad because
it means less business and fewer jobs.

People in countries with poor economies can make more money
selling tiger parts than from taking part in conservation efforts. If
they have to choose between feeding their families and protecting
the tigers, the tigers will always lose. These are just some of the
things that make tiger conservation an ongoing challenge.

Without help from humans, it is possible that in the future, tigers will only be found in captivity.

Efforts to rescue tigers from a final fate are not just the responsibility of countries or organizations. Individuals do their part, too. One of the most important keys to saving the tigers is education. Conservationists petition governments, give speeches, write books, and run Web sites about the risk of tiger extinction. Through these actions, they hope that others will not buy tiger products and may even contribute time or money to conservation programs. Gradually, these steps help improve the tigers' chances.

Statistics indicate that some tigers, such as the Siberian, are making a comeback. Their numbers are increasing. But until more of their habitat is preserved and illegal tiger activity is stopped, their situation remains fragile. Tigers are adaptable animals capable of mighty acts, but they will not be able to save themselves.

GLOSSARY

camouflage—To hide by blending in.

captivity—For animals, not living in the wild. Being kept or born as a pet or in a zoo, sanctuary, or wildlife preserve.

carcass—The body of a dead animal.

conservation—The act of preserving or protecting something.

cub—A baby tiger.

deforestation—The act of removing trees.

extinct—No longer existing.

pests—Organisms that are seen as a nuisance or bothersome to people.

poacher—A person who illegally hunts animals.

predator—An animal that hunts other animals.

preserve—An area where wild animals live under human protection; can also be called a reserve.

prey—An animal that is hunted.

species—A specific type of animal. A tiger is a species of big cat.

stealth—The act of moving or doing something quietly and carefully without attracting attention.

vegetation—Trees and other plant life.

FIND OUT MORE

Books

Bortolotti, Dan, *Tiger Rescue: Changing the Future for Endangered Wildlife*. Ontario, Canada: Firefly Books, 2003.

Hirschi, Ron. *Lions, Tigers, and Bears: Why Are Big Predators So Rare?* Honesdale, PA: Boyds Mills Press, 2007.

Kalman, Bobbie. *Endangered Tigers*. New York: Crabtree Publishing, 2004.

Spilsbury, Richard. *Bengal Tiger*. Chicago: Heinemann Library, 2004.

Stone, Lynn M.*Tigers*. Minneapolis, MN: Carolrhoda Books, 2005.

Web Sites

Cyber Tiger
http://magma.nationalgeographic.com/ngexplorer/0311/adventures

Defenders of Wildlife: Tiger
http://www.defenders.org/wildlife_and_habitat/wildlife/tiger.php

Indian Tiger Welfare Society
http://www.indiantiger.org

National Geographic: Tigers
http://www.nationalgeographic.com/kids/creature_feature/0012/
tigers.html

World Wildlife Fund: Tigers
http://www.panda.org/about_wwf/what_we_do/species/about_
species/species_factsheets/tigers/index.cfm

Organizations

Save the Tiger Fund
The National Fish and Wildlife Foundation
1120 Connecticut Avenue, NW, Suite 900
Washington D.C. 20036
Phone: (202) 857-0166
http://www.savethetigerfund.org

World Wildlife Fund
1250 Twenty-Fourth Street, N.W.
P.O. Box 97180
Washington, DC 20090-7180
Phone: (202) 293-4800
http://www.worldwildlife.org

ABOUT THE AUTHOR

Marc Tyler Nobleman has written more than sixty books for young people and one for adults. His titles include *Vocabulary Cartoon of the Day*, *What's the Difference?*, and *365 Adventures*. He also writes regularly for *Nickelodeon Magazine*.

INDEX

Pages numbers in **boldface** are illustrations.